For Roberta

Text copyright © 2013 by Diane E. Muldrow
All interior illustrations copyright © by Random House, Inc.
All rights reserved.
Published in the United States by Golden Books, an imprint of Random House Children's
Books, a division of Random House, Inc., 1745 Broadway, New York, NY 10019.
Golden Books, A Golden Book, A Little Golden Book, the G colophon, and the distinctive
gold spine are registered trademarks of Random House, Inc. The Little Red Hen,
The Saggy Baggy Elephant, Scuffy the Tugboat, The Shy Little Kitten, Tawny Scrawny Lion,
and Tootle are trademarks of Random House, Inc. The Poky Little Puppy
is a registered trademark of Random House, Inc.
Good Humor® trademarks and logos are used with permission of Good Humor-Breyers
Ice Cream.
The artwork contained in this work was previously published in separate works
by Golden Books, New York.

Cover photograph copyright © 2001 British Photographers' Liaison Committee/Finers Stephens.

randomhouse.com
dianemuldrow.com
Library of Congress Control Number: 2012949414

ISBN 978-0-307-97761-8 (trade) — ISBN 978-0-375-97126-6 (lib. bdg) — ISBN 978-0-375-98118-0 (ebook)
Printed in the United States of America
10

Everything I Need to Know I Learned From a Little Golden Book

DIANE MULDROW

g A GOLDEN BOOK • NEW YORK

Dear Reader,

    If you are like most Americans, you grew up with Little Golden Books—or Big Golden Books or Giant Golden Books. You were tantalized by the rows of colorful cardboard covers in a rack at the drugstore or variety store showing pictures of a feisty little tugboat, a train, or a certain little brown-and-white puppy. Perhaps someone who loved you placed a brand-new Little Golden Book on your coverlet when you came down with a case of the collywobbles. Maybe your mother handed you one to keep you occupied in the seat of the wire cart as she pushed you down the aisles of the supermarket. You lovingly ran your finger along the shiny gold foil glued to the spine, and when you got the book home, you proudly scrawled your name on the inside front cover, where it said:

This Little Golden Book belongs to

We at Golden Books think there's a good chance that many of us learned pretty much everything that really matters about life from what we read between those sturdy, gilt-bound cardboard covers. It's true!

Our country has faced some hard times of late, and we've been forced to look at ourselves and how we're living our lives. Ironically, in this health-conscious, ecologically aware age of information, many of us have overborrowed, overspent, overeaten, and generally overdosed on habits or ways of life that aren't good for us—or for our world. The chickens have come home to roost, and their names are Debt, Depression, and Diabetes.

How did we get here? How, like Tootle the Train, did we get so off track? Perhaps it's time to revisit these beloved stories and start all over again. Trying to figure out where you belong, like Scuffy the Tugboat? Maybe, as time marches on, you're beginning to feel that you resemble the Saggy Baggy Elephant.

Or perhaps your problems are more sweeping. Like the Poky Little Puppy, do you seem to be getting into trouble rather often and missing out on the strawberry shortcake in life? Maybe this book can help you! After all, Little Golden Books were first published during the dark days of World War II, and they've been comforting people during trying times ever since—while gently teaching us a thing or two. And they remind us that we've had the potential to be wise and content all along.

Diane Muldrow

Diane Muldrow is a longtime editorial director at Golden Books and a prolific author of books for children.

From *Circus Time* by Marion Conger, illustrated by Tibor Gergely, 1948.

Is your life starting to feel
like a circus?

Don't panic. . . .

From *The Seven Sneezes* by Olga Cabral, illustrated by Tibor Gergely, 1948.

Today's a new day!

From *Good Morning and Good Night* by Jane Werner, illustrated by Eloise Wilkin, 1949.

Get dressed first thing.

(Sweatpants are bad for morale. Put on something nice!)

Top: from *Lucky Mrs. Ticklefeather* by Dorothy Kunhardt, illustrated by J. P. Miller, 1951.
Bottom: from *The Happy Family* by Nicole, illustrated by Corinne Malvern, 1955.

Have some pancakes.

From *Duck and His Friends* by Kathryn and Byron Jackson, illustrated by Richard Scarry, 1949.

Get some exercise every day.

From *Animal Gym* by Beth Greiner Hoffman,
illustrated by Tibor Gergely, 1956.

Frolic.

From *Tootle* by Gertrude Crampton, illustrated by Tibor Gergely, 1945.

Daydream.

From *I Can Fly* by Ruth Krauss, illustrated by Mary Blair, 1951.

Go on a joyride!

From *Tommy's Wonderful Rides* by Helen Palmer, illustrated by J. P. Miller, 1948.

Stargaze. . . .

From *The Friendly Book* by Margaret Wise Brown, illustrated by Garth Williams, 1954.

Stroll.

From *The Three Bears*, illustrated by Feodor Rojankovsky, 1948.

Bird-watch.

From *I Am a Bunny*, A Golden Sturdy Book, by Ole Risom, illustrated by Richard Scarry, 1963.

From *The Good Humor Man* by Kathleen N. Daly,
illustrated by Tibor Gergely, 1964.

Treat yourself.

SPECIAL TODAY

Good Humor ICE CREAM

The simplest things are often the most fun!

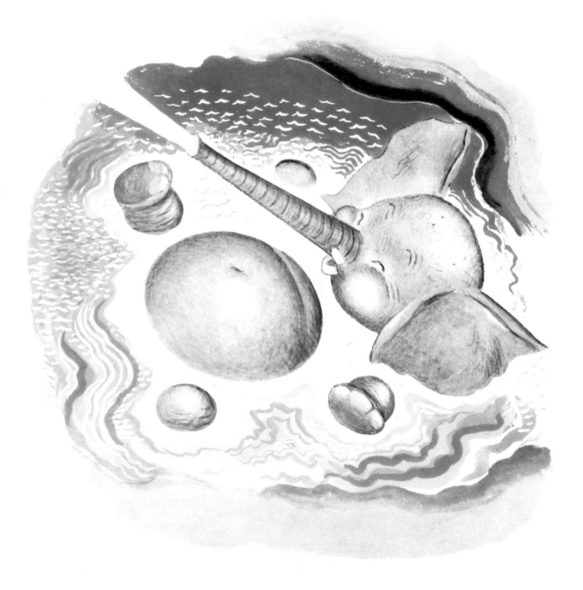

From *The Saggy Baggy Elephant* by Kathryn and Byron Jackson, illustrated by Gustaf Tenggren, 1947.

So go on a picnic . . .

From *Duck and His Friends* by Kathryn and Byron Jackson, illustrated by Richard Scarry, 1949.

and make music a part of your life.

From *The Musicians of Bremen*, adapted from Jacob and Wilhelm Grimm, illustrated by J. P. Miller, 1954.

Be a hugger.

From *Georgie Finds a Grandpa* by Miriam Young,
illustrated by Eloise Wilkin, 1954.

Kiss.

From *The Happy Family* by Nicole, illustrated by Gertrude Elliott, 1947.

**Turn off the TV
from time to time . . .**

From *Naughty Bunny*, written and illustrated by Richard Scarry, 1959.

and crack open a book!

From *Baby's First Book* by Garth Williams, 1955.

Use your imagination.

From *Nurse Nancy* by Kathryn Jackson, illustrated by Corinne Malvern, 1952.

Look up . . .

From *My Little Golden Book About God* by Jane Werner Watson, illustrated by Eloise Wilkin, 1956.

and savor the seasons as they roll around.

From *I Am a Bunny*, A Golden Sturdy Book, by Ole Risom, illustrated by Richard Scarry, 1963.

Stay curious.

From *Baby Listens* by Esther Wilkin, illustrated by Eloise Wilkin, 1960.

Take in some culture once in a while.

From *Daddies* by Janet Frank, illustrated by Tibor Gergely, 1953.

Learn something new!

From *Tootle* by Gertrude Crampton, illustrated by Tibor Gergely, 1945.

Dare to explore.
What's out there for you?

From *The Sailor Dog* by Margaret Wise Brown, illustrated by Garth Williams, 1953.

Express yourself.

From *Daddies* by Janet Frank, illustrated by Tibor Gergely, 1953.

Try a new look!

From *Pantaloon* by Kathryn Jackson, illustrated by Leonard Weisgard, 1951.

Be unique.

From *Rupert the Rhinoceros* by Carl Memling, illustrated by Tibor Gergely, 1960.

Just don't go overboard.

From *The Seven Sneezes* by Olga Cabral, illustrated by Tibor Gergely, 1948.

Start planning that dream trip!

From *Open Up My Suitcase* by Alice Low, illustrated by Corinne Malvern, 1954.

Soon you'll be on your way.

From *All Aboard!* by Marion Conger, illustrated by Corinne Malvern, 1952.

Be open to making new friends . . .

From *The Shy Little Kitten* by Cathleen Schurr, illustrated by Gustaf Tenggren, 1946.

even if you're very, very shy.

Keep in touch.

From *Seven Little Postmen* by Margaret Wise Brown and Edith Thacher Hurd, illustrated by Tibor Gergely, 1952.

Hang out.

Top: from *Tootle* by Gertrude Crampton, illustrated by Tibor Gergely, 1945.
Bottom: from *A Day on the Farm* by Nancy Fielding Hulick, illustrated by J. P. Miller, 1960.

Steer clear of shady characters.

From *Chicken Little*, adapted by Vivienne Benstead, illustrated by Richard Scarry, 1960.

Be discriminating.

From *Daddies* by Janet Frank, illustrated by Tibor Gergely, 1953.

Choose your companions wisely.

From *The Gingerbread Man*
by Nancy Nolte,
illustrated by
Richard Scarry, 1953.

Break bread together every day.

From *Mister Dog* by Margaret Wise Brown, illustrated by Garth Williams, 1952.

Don't forget your antioxidants!

From *The Color Kittens* by Margaret Wise Brown, illustrated by Alice and Martin Provensen, 1949.

**Go ahead and make a big deal
over your birthday.**

From *Chipmunk's ABC* by Roberta Miller, illustrated by Richard Scarry, 1963.

Dress up and go dancing . . .

From *The Twelve Dancing Princesses* by the Brothers Grimm, retold by Jane Werner, illustrated by Sheilah Beckett, 1954.

any kind of dancing!

From *The Saggy Baggy Elephant* by Kathryn and Byron Jackson, illustrated by Gustaf Tenggren, 1947.

Make something from nothing.

From *The Party Pig* by Kathryn and Byron Jackson, illustrated by Richard Scarry, 1954.

Sing even if you can't hold a tune.

From *Nursery Songs*, arranged by Leah Gale, illustrated by Corinne Malvern, 1942.

Learn to cook . . .

From *We Help Mommy* by Jean Cushman, illustrated by Eloise Wilkin, 1959.

and clean!

From *Animal Friends* by Jane Werner, illustrated by Garth Williams, 1953.

**Make a budget—
and stick to it!**

From *5 Pennies to Spend* by Miriam Young, illustrated by Corinne Malvern, 1955.

**Have you had
a checkup
lately?**

From *Tommy Visits the Doctor* by Jean H. Seligmann and Milton I. Levine, MD,
illustrated by Richard Scarry, 1962.

Weren't you going to learn how to swim?

From *The Little Fat Policeman* by Margaret Wise Brown and Edith Thacher Hurd,
illustrated by Alice and Martin Provensen, 1950.

Always keep a medical kit handy.

From *Nurse Nancy* by Kathryn Jackson, illustrated by Corinne Malvern, 1952.

Cultivate contentment.

From *Tawny Scrawny Lion* by Kathryn Jackson, illustrated by Gustaf Tenggren, 1952.

Take a mental health day
now and then.

From *The Little Red Hen*, illustrated by J. P. Miller, 1954.

Give in to a good cry.
You'll feel better afterward!

From *My Little Golden Book About God* by Jane Werner Watson, illustrated by Eloise Wilkin, 1956.

Get plenty of
sleep, too.

From *The Little Red Hen*, illustrated by J. P. Miller, 1954.

Go fly a kite . . .

From *Chicken Little*, adapted by Vivienne Benstead, illustrated by Richard Scarry, 1960.

but remember to stop
and smell the strawberries.

From *The Poky Little Puppy* by Janette Sebring Lowrey, illustrated by Gustaf Tenggren, 1942.

Be a romantic.

From *The Blue Book of Fairy Tales*,
illustrated by Gordon Laite, 1959.

Don't forget to enjoy your wedding!

From *The Paper Doll Wedding* by Hilda Miloche and Wilma Kane, 1954.

From *Baby Dear* by Esther Wilkin, illustrated by Eloise Wilkin, 1962.

Let your children know you love them.

Work hard.

From *Daddies* by Janet Frank, illustrated by Tibor Gergely, 1953.

Play hard.

From *Mister Dog*
by Margaret Wise Brown,
illustrated by Garth Williams, 1952.

But not *too* hard.

From *Animal Stories*, a Giant Golden Book, by Georges Duplaix, illustrated by Feodor Rojankovsky, 1944.

Do no harm.

From *My Little Golden Book About God* by Jane Werner Watson, illustrated by Eloise Wilkin, 1956.

Be proud of your country.

From *Our Flag* by Carl Memling, illustrated by Stephen Cook, 1960.

Don't let the parade
pass you by!

From *Here Comes the Parade* by Kathryn Jackson, illustrated by Richard Scarry, 1951.

Think big!

From *Little Peewee: Or Now Open the Box* by Dorothy Kunhardt, illustrated by J. P. Miller, 1948.

Toot your own horn!

From *Little Boy with a Big Horn* by Jack Bechdolt, illustrated by Aurelius Battaglia, 1950.

Harvest.

From *Two Little Gardeners* by Margaret Wise Brown and Edith Thacher Hurd, illustrated by
Gertrude Elliott, 1951.

Give thanks.

From *Prayers for Children,* illustrated by Eloise Wilkin, 1952.

Believe in Santa Claus . . .

From *The Night Before Christmas* by Clement C. Moore, illustrated by Corinne Malvern, 1949.

love at first sight . . .

From *The House That Jack Built*, illustrated by J. P. Miller, 1954.

From *Boats* by Ruth Mabee Lachman, illustrated by Lenora and Herbert Combes, 1951.

and that your ship will come in.
As long as you do, your life is bound to be Golden!